T0269813

HAPPY POEMS
and
OTHER LIES

by JEDDIE SOPHRONIUS

CODHILL
PRESS

ABOUT THE AUTHOR

Jeddie Sophronius is the author of the poetry collections *Interrogation Records* (Gaudy Boy, 2024), *Love & Sambal* (The Word Works, 2024), and the chapbook *Blood•Letting* (Quarterly West, 2023). A Chinese-Indonesian writer from Jakarta, they received their MFA from the University of Virginia, where they currently serve as a lecturer in English. The recipient of the 2023 Gaudy Boy Poetry Book Prize, their poems have appeared in *The Cincinnati Review, The Iowa Review, Prairie Schooner,* and elsewhere. Read more of their work at nakedcentaur.com

HAPPY POEMS
and
OTHER LIES

C

CODHILL PRESS
NEW YORK · NEW PALTZ

CODHILL
PRESS

codhill.com

HAPPY POEMS AND OTHER LIES Copyright © 2024
JEDDIE SOPHRONIUS

Published in the United States of America

ISBN 978-1-949933-26-0
Library of Congress Control Number: 2024934097

Cover and Book Design by Jana Potashnik
BAIRDesign · bairdesign.com

FOR MY FAMILY

CONTENTS

I

For Jesus Himself testified that a prophet hath no honor in his own country.

—John 4:44

SONG OF THE PROPHET

the rulers can't explain the suffering
that exist why the gods
remain lost and
unmoved as they hear the hungry birds.
witness the foals in a prophecy:
sparrows singing, we live
today we survive in our cold
bodies in cages, forever
neglected by this city— in need of
rice. maybe we can mold a prophet
up in heaven, a messiah to move
ignorant gods and start calming the oceans

HERITAGE

Like a good son, I stole my
    mother's
insomnia when she delivered me.

My cries kept the neighborhood
    awake.
The night wind was my sunlight, the chorus

of birds my signal to sleep.
    I grew
up believing I was a sinner. By

age nine, my record was one
    warm night
without sleep. I could say it was my first

high—the visible world a
    pool of
water in which I could baptize myself

to sleep. By nineteen, it was
    three days.
What did I do? The same things I did when

I was sleeping: I carried
    on with
my days, walked three hours to the nearest

  mountain, visited zebras,
 lions,
and chimpanzees in their fake habitat.

  I sensed they weren't sleeping too.
 Lunches
blurred into dinners, dinners were just snacks.

  When I told the church of the
 symptom
that runs in my family, I was told

  to pray more. Repent. Read Psalms.
 Twenty-
nine: five days without a meal or sleep. I

  believed those who said my sleep-
 lessness
was the wage of my sins. I was closest

  to God then, mouthing verses
 every
night instead of sleep. A prophet I could

  have been—all the visions I've
 seen—but
who would believe me?

CONFESSION

father   I don't remember
the last time I wrote   a letter to God

but I do recall   that Sunday when you
preached all nightmares are   the dead

telling us to confess
    thus *they are all God-sent*
    thus *confess confess*

father   I would kneel with you in prayer
if only   you were here

you talk of ghosts   as though
you know them   but you've miscalled my name

for a child no longer here   for the twelfth time now
have you forgotten   I've come home?

yes I'm no longer the boy   who packed his lunch
in a kitchen   full of empty bottles

and I know my sleeplessness
is a symptom   of my sins

but maybe it is a symptom
of yours too   father

it's all right   just lay your head down
    close your eyes

do not fear   the voices
I know   your regrets

can last generations   but
now is your time to listen

GOSPEL OF THE UNSETTLED PROPHET

Dear Lord of Heaven / and Untimely Miracles / it's not
that I don't believe in You / I'd offer this life to a well if I
must / heave a bucket out of it / every morning even in the
winter / but which well is the question / You have yet to lie
me down / in green pastures beside quiet waters / it's cold
out here and all I hear / is the song of this rusty pulley / no
shepherd to find this / body who wandered from the flock
/ no language to say anything / without spitting a wool of
accent / what should I say when someone asks me / where
I'm from or what / I'm doing I'm nowhere like You / God
of human beings with perfect skin / this lost sparrow has
yet to decide / an answer how about this / I crawled from a
shattered well / lost pieces of my faith along the way / I'm
trying to find the rest / one bucket at a time / look now / I
see a child rising from the water

A PROPHET WITHOUT WORDS

after Mai Der Vang

God told me to scissor the night
to practice my vowels.

>After *bisa* comes *Isa* comes *kisah,*
>after poison comes Jesus comes a tale.

>After *padi* comes *beras* comes *nasi,*
>after rice comes rice comes rice.

My faith wreathes into a red scarf
a refugee wears, for it smells like home.

>The washing instructions say:
>If one cannot divide,
>one must go across the Red Sea.

Years ago, I was a son who came home
bringing bread every day.

>*Ramah* leads to *marah* leads to *remah,*
>kindness leads to anger leads to crumbs.

Looking across the sea,
I left my sack of rice back home.

SONG OF THE SPARROW

Once an eternity, a sparrow sings
hallelujah. Every dozen hallelujahs
    or more, a sparrow is born a Messiah
and a four-year-old unlocks its cage, opens all
    the windows. Before I was a son, I
was a star, then an angel, lost in a dive bar,

    looking for his father. Now I can't fly
back to heaven, my wings are tied to a dead tree.
    I hop along the way to the bus stop
hugging bags of groceries. Again, my mother,
    is singing how many songs now? She says

maybe I will have a baby sister. When it
    comes to Messiahs, we don't know how long they
have traveled, how tired they are from all the moving.
    Sometimes, a house has no windows at all.

The first time I tried gin, I mistook it as a
    sign for flight. Someone left all the windows
open, someone guilty of not singing. I am

    tired of moving from city to city,
my father is still nowhere. What do you call a

    sparrow whose wings are nailed to a dead tree?

CONVERSATION WITH A
BLEEDING GOD IN MY ARMS

I wear red and white
The flag of my country
I am not white
I want to go home early
I can't move from where I am
With a bleeding God in my arms
I look around
I don't see anyone
I'm not a doctor
Just say grace
Lord,
Thank you for this gathering—
I don't think that's how this works
Stay with me until I die
How long do stars take to explode?
You smell like chamomile and porridge
Please take me with You?
Do you believe in me?
I'm not sure
Will I see You again?
I have questions about the Bible
I highlighted the contradictions
I didn't write it
My mother is calling
She won't like seeing me
Talking to a bleeding stranger
Tell her I'm God
I don't know who to forgive
My sister or my childhood bully
Forgive both
I need to feed my dog

CONVERSATION WITH THE DEVIL

I've never been to heaven
but I descend to hell knowing God
is nowhere in sight. The dirt is cold
like kisses of a dying mother and there is no ceiling.

What's the opposite of claustrophobia?
The devil arrives holding a round mirror
next to his head. *Remember me?*
Of course, I do, I know my own face

when I see one, and right now, there are two.
He says my hair reminds him
of his days flying in heaven.
He shows me the nails piercing

the purple veins of his featherless wings.
I wonder who prays for him.
He dances around as his bloody nails
leave their trails on my naked body.

Do I make you agoraphobic?
Yes, that's the word. I believe
it's only agoraphobic
when you're with strangers.

I realize that sounds romantic.
I hope he doesn't fall in love with me,
he's suffered enough.
I'm here to take my lover's place, I tell him.

He grins like a child about to win—
he always likes to bargain.
You don't have a lover.
Yes. In the eyes of the church,

I'm just an obedient prophet
who never know what it's like to be naked
in front of another pair of eyes,
who never know the two differences of

love: one sounds like rust,
and the other sounds like a bride's heels
as she runs away with a different man.
But I haven't been to church lately.

How can you take your lover's place,
if you have no home to offer?
Here, take my hair.
Pull out every single strand from my body.

I pray you'll fly again.

MATTHEW 18:9

When my father's friends ask me why I don't
want to be a pastor like my father
I tell them, my father's seat in heaven
is so high, I can't see his face, even

when he's at home. I tell them I don't like
wine, bowing my head, and listening to
people's problems. I have enough jasmine
tea at home to last until the Rapture.

Like Joseph, I tell them my dreams, the dreams
I call visions, they're almost biblical:
I dream of the old men who visited
and sexualized my sister one eye too

many, I dream of shattering their wine
glasses, gouging their eyes to save their soul.

BLACK HOLE

When my classmate calls my country a shithole,
I laugh with him. I don't know what *shithole* means.
He takes my laughter as a sign of my agreement.
He parades me, the new kid, as an exhibition
for the other white kids to see. My plaque says, *from shithole.*

Lunch break after lunch break, new visitors arrive
bearing questions: *Does your country have electricity?*
Do your people eat dogs? Did you come here by boat?
With each new question, I form an accent. I try
to speak the way they did, heavy and fast, but my tongue

stumbles over my words. Sometimes, my visitors
leave before I get the chance to answer them.
Soon, the whole school becomes familiar with my brownness,
my exhibition no longer new. They get bored of me.

Year after year, I still rehearse my answers.
When do I say my name? When do I say *shithole?*
Shithole, asshole, black hole. So many holes
in my English. So many holes in my throat.
How do I chew a language

without coughing up another? Say instead, *I'm Jd,*
Two letters. No accent at all. No one
needs to hear my mother's tongue.
Forget, *aku.* Forget, *saya,* Forget *gue.*
Say, *I.* Say, *me.* Say, *Jd.*

PILGRIMAGE

Everywhere I went, strangers asked me where I'm from,
prickled me with their questions, their *just wonderings*—
they reminded me I'll never be one of them.

At grade school in Australia, a kid threw gum
at my hair. The others laughed at my suffering.
Everywhere I went, strangers asked me where I'm from.

High school in Indonesia: I was a bookworm
who struggled speaking. Kids laughed at my stuttering.
They reminded me I'll never be one of them.

At twenty-one, my whole family called me dumb
for dropping out. I left home, started wandering.
Everywhere I went, strangers asked me where I'm from.

For a while, I walked until a friend housed this bum;
his friends laughed, after asking about my earnings.
They reminded me I'll never be one of them.

Every city has its own laughers, its own thorns.
I was always going somewhere, always walking.
They reminded me I'll never be one of them.
Everywhere I went, strangers asked me where I'm from.

WHEN I ASK THE BIBLE

When I ask the Bible
scholar for work, she says,
"You have no love for God
or His people, only
money." She speaks the truth.
For a second, I can

imagine a future
where I knock on church doors,
asking for hymnal books
to dust or sermons to
transcribe. I remembered
the holy waters years

ago, pouring over
me when I was a babe:
untouched by the need for
money, still cradled by
my mother, every night,
until I said goodbye

to bad dreams. But now my
nightmares have returned so
hungry, they drive a spear
through my belly—and since
then I too have become
hungry like the devils.

MEDITATION: A MEMORY

In the stillness of night, I listened to whispers in the air—
praying to no particular god now, no longer my father's heir.

My faith kept shrinking until it was a ball that fit my pocket,
a reminder of a past life, one where I had Samson's hair.

Back then, exorcism was a weekly routine. The church leaders
laid hands on me—made me confess at the altar, for all to hear.

My father knew what was happening, yet did nothing. Played dumb
to hide that dark secret of the religion. Pretended there was no err

If there is a father, I don't know what to say to him.
I've always been jaded, never knowing why I'm here.

FATHER, FORGIVE ME

for I'm single, the youngest son, the prophesied
prophet—I've failed to continue the family
line. My hands are talons, too birdlike and bloody

to use the chopsticks at the dining table. How
can I convince anyone to marry me? I
prefer men and women who tolerate someone

eating a fistful of rice with bare hands. I know,
there's mud under my fingernails. And yes, every
sin committed is a sparrow crying, and yes,

I'm single until it's convenient for you
to die, for my name to be crossed off from our
family certificate. Sometimes I open

my mouth and a wolf comes out. Sometimes that wolf is
you, father. When you howl, I get tired, afraid.
How long should I wait before I sweep the rubbles

in the kitchen, the broken plates and wasted rice?
father, forgive me for I know not what to do
with all these sparrows you've entrusted in my arms.

DOGMA

Here, a sparrow
the One
God has forgotten
to watch over
like sheep,
and here,
a shepherd,
trying to calm
their wailings,
their silence.
the Pharisees stared at
a bruised boy trying to sell
his cowl of
a sinful creature,

and a boy, who didn't know
who died for our sins, and
the proverbial words of
Eden, where the sparrows were
inside the cave with
a voice,
an imitation of
the raging oceans.
in the darkness
the people worshipped
the Golden Calf
a garment of
shame spoke of a priest
who never knew what it's like to be

a King,
he said,
men who had
flocked
the burning bush
of
God,
with their sandals on,
are the same as
the bystanders,
who stood by as
the Lord, fell silent...
as if he were
crucified.

II

Every prophet grows sick and tired

of prophesying

— Kei Miller, "Book of Jonah"

CITY OF LOST

It's no one's fault if the cartographers
think the number of islands keeps changing.

    White cays and rocky reefs appear
           during low tide,

                then sleep with the seahorses
                  under the moonlit waters.

I have walked along streets
named after islands.

      In this city, no one knows I'm here,
    I come home and leave before anyone notices.

                Yes, we all look the same
                under the shadow of the skyscrapers.

I only visit to smell my old books
and run my fingers along the cracks in my bedroom walls,

      the cement dust has covered
    any traces of childhood.

Each year, the cracks grow longer,
and the pattern looks like the surface of a distant planet—
wrinkled with the loneliness of missing a child.

CONVERSATION WITH SNOW

Snow, why are you heartless?

Must I apologize for my mother,
for speaking a language you are not

accustomed to hearing? Is it
because of her curved, oriental eyes,
the way she gets her *I's* and *E's* mixed up?

Does the way her old hands drag
the grocery bags home at night
make it tempting for cold to settle?
Which is it, snow? When my dog died

we put him in a sack and dug a hole.
There is no funeral for an offering.
What must we bury in you, snow? A sister
I never met? An absent father? Anyone, please,
but my mother. You don't know what it takes

for her to come here, her back almost broken
because of the sack she still carries. She didn't
come here just for a bunch of churchgoers to snicker
at her because she needs to go to the bathroom
every five hallelujahs or so. Snow, you're not
Abraham, there's no God telling you to do this.

The last time she met you, she wept in her sleep
for six years. Whose name was it that kept popping up

>

in her prayers? Now I know, snow. I know why
my mother doesn't come out of her room
in the winter, why she looks outside her window
and has the tears of someone who can never forgive
the stranger who took away her baby's life.

WHEN I CAME HOME

My nephew asked, "How did it feel to live in the snow?"
Felt like I was naked all the time.

Mother said she was fasting. Gave my sister
two slices of apple for breakfast. Told her to say grace anyway.

One of our own just got mugged last night.
A young girl.

It could have been worse.

My social media inbox was still full of unanswered messages.
Nobody realized I was away.

A stranger on the internet argued that Orientals tend to be
attracted to whites.
Not the other way around.

My old friend teased, "How can you still see with those small
eyes?"

A wooden cart full of rubbish. A father and son sleeping
on a cardboard bed. Nothing but their cracked hands as
pillows
    and the night, their blanket.

This was the sight of home back then, the sight of home now.

>

In the family prayer, my mother was grateful her son was still alive.

My father said his prayer in broken English.

I spoke mine in birdsongs and open wounds.

CONVERSATION WITH THE EMPTY GARDEN

Do you remember the day father swung
his rusted axe with the shaky handle?
The family dog almost died, and the tree,
the axe was intended for, fell not long

after. What happened to the dachshund whose
belly had no fur? The blue deer who came
to drink by the fish pond every night? *Child,
come see.* In the city, mother and I

window-shopped all the stuff we couldn't buy:
raspberries, ice cream, a phone call to home.
Plastic plants reminded us of the rose
bed in our font yard, back home. Did we leave

behind a prophet on our way back? Like
Adam, I too, miss the garden of my
childhood. I never got the chance to say
goodbye. *Honey, we miss you all the time.*

So do I. I miss the childhood I never had,
glimpses of what could've been.

ALTAR

My English teacher once said, don't start a sentence with *because,* because you will likely end up with a fragment. Something will go missing. A Lego piece, grandpa's towel, or a noun, like father. Still, I refuse to follow directions. I don't want to ask for help. I stumble my way through my childhood bedroom that has now turned too dark to see. I call out the same person in different languages, hoping to get an answer. *Ayah, Baba, Abba.* When my eyes have adjusted to the darkness, I can see that the scribblings I've made years ago have been painted clean. My old toys have been thrown away along with the family photographs. I believe if you wait long enough a shadow will turn into something you no longer remember, like the rose you plucked and tucked around your father's ear when you were five. Someday, I will understand my mother's words: *Some things are more beautiful when they are missing.*

RAINY SEASON

I never asked to be a river

but my family needed a basin

Their tears after my sister's funeral

flowed like melted snow, a mountain spring

Puddles, ponds, pools, the water falls, coursed

formed tributaries and mouthed me

As the water gathered in the clouds

of my childhood, I caught each raindrop

all the *hallelujahs* and *fuck yous*

let them all pass through as good rivers

would do. But this river could only

contain so much. When rainy season

arrived, I would flood, fail to hold all

the water

TIDE

Someone left a baby
at the mouth of a watery cave.
Bundled in white, the small
creature's cries a kitten
asking for attention. But there
was only the moon. And echoes.
Echoes, loud enough for the whole
village to hear. Candles blown out, doors
locked, bananas fell from their tree.
In another life, there was no cave, only
a priest baptizing an infant, water
pouring down from his small head
back to the golden bowl, again and again.
It's easier to think of death this way—
an offering, life ending so early. We
don't have to understand: a father
locks the bathroom and cries; a priest
loses his faith; a mother refuses
to meet her son's choice of partner;
and the son runs, to the cave that knows
his name. O Lord, raise the tide now,
your offering awaits its ascension.

REBIRTH

My sister died. I didn't. We never met.
Mother locked the door every time
she came home. I was afraid
of dead children, dark mirrors,
my nakedness. Once, someone said, *I wish*

it was you. Once, I set myself on fire:
my hair seared as fast as dried leaves, the loose ends
smelled like burned cockroaches. I died
and saw my sister. How she aged beautifully.
She didn't remember who I was, didn't know.

My sister died and never came back. The lungs
in her small body collapsed like old roofs.
The doctors pumped morphine, bag after bag,
until she couldn't feel mother's touch. Her casket
was no larger than a shoebox. I found no instruction

on what to do at the cemetery. But I found
my sister, sleeping. I lie beside her until I
was born of tears and empty bottles. Mother,
I'm still here. Do you still see your daughter
slipping away from your arms every time you sleep?

FAMILY HISTORY

New year, a son returns from self-imposed
exile, traces his name along the dust-
filled makeshift bed: a sleeping bag, wooden

plank, a backpack as pillow. As long as
you have roof, you should be grateful, he was
taught. The roof is collapsing, has collapsed:

light bulb bursting with the rainwater, shards
floating on flooded floors. Like a river-
bed, a bedroom can contain only so

much water. To live here, one remains un-
touched by sleep and silence. Even childhood
has forgotten this place. I can only

remain away for so long before I
fall forgotten from the family tree.

When my father's sins were laid before me
I asked the empty bottles of whisky,
"Have you seen my father?"

"No," they replied.
Their round bellies reflect my confusion.

I asked the men magazines, pills,
and religious self-help books. I asked his
priesthood, "Are you my father?"

"No, I am a mask
he wears for the world."   >

I find the backyard newly dug, our old
dog nowhere to be found. I find mother
still bedridden, her coughs echo through the

living room. What is a face, if not to
remind us of childhood? I remember
the first time I left, when mother carried

me through immigration, holding her scared
son in one hand, passports in another.
If I could ask for one thing, I would ask

for more time together, more childhood. I
would consider, even for a moment,
if I made the right choice of leaving.

They interrogated me. Asked me where I'm from. Forgot,
then asked again. Told me I misspelled my name.
Told me I'm not welcome here. They wrote my history.
Told me my ancestors were traitors.
Asked me why I'm not fair-skinned. Told me I was
different.   >

No greetings for me this time: no surprise
hugs from behind, no crying mother who
thinks she's in a dream, no old high school friends

coming to visit. I drink to the ghost
of my past—my dead ancestors, my dead
childhood—every night. It's the only way

to still their laughter. Don't worry,
it's no one fault but my own
that I'm the only one still alive.

A recurring dream: running through the airport
corridors, out of breath, my sack in hand. And each time

I reached my gate, they never let me in. I watched
my plane took off without me, and with it, my home.

FATHER ABECEDARIAN

After all this time,
believe me or not, my return still
causes you inconvenience: you have to set up a
desk, mattress, and pillows
elevated out of dusty self-help books.
Fine, I no longer have my own room and
given my departure, I can't find my violin.
How long before you blame me for sleeping with a Muslim girl?
I guess home is a purgatory where fathers need to offer
just their children's rooms in exchange for heaven.
Knowing nothing, this pillow says: *To forgive, one must say out
loud, one must pronounce "father" properly.* Yes,
my home is a sculpture of my past, a childhood song I
no longer remember. In this shelter of a sunken temple
only by submerging myself to sleep, could I find my body
praying to the face of a drowned God.
Question after question befalls me, the tide
rises and I remember this God; He
sank when He crossed the oceans to find my mother.
Thus, He prays with His eyes as though they were
under the possession of the Holy Spirit.
Violin strings vibrate, echoing above the surface. The
water parts, disintegrates, dries up.
Xenophobia turns unveiled without the water of the verses.
You can see now, this God, He is made of stone,
zealous to remain dry amid all this water.

MY FATHER TRIES TO SING

With each strum of chords
the tips of his fingers
                    turn red against the strings.

> *I learned this*
> *when grandpa was in prison.*

A quiet sigh. His head bowing down.
The melody on repeat.

I lay my head on the bedroom floor
so I can see his face.

> But the tune flows differently,
> like how the edge of a stream
>   turns into a waterfall.

He coughs somewhere between
a thousand ships and a painting of home.

His hair has grown
        white since I last saw him.

                    Wrinkles on his cheeks.

            The waterfall freezes.

He says doesn't remember how the rest goes,

pats my sleepy head instead,
rests the guitar against the wall

and leaves.

He coughs again.

So I wait.
I wait for him to remember.

NIGHTLY PRAYER

It is a sin to pray for our dead,
my mother said, *your grandpa, aunt, sister,*

they're no longer your concern. I learned
what is permitted, what is forbidden.

During our nightly prayer, mother shaped
my unsteady hands into a shy plant.

I closed myself for an invisible
father, out of fear for the visible

mother in front of me. I stayed silent
during this ritual, a good flower

I was: never speaking, just listening.
One night, I heard a secret, my mother

praying for a forbidden name, *Dagna,*
a name I've learned not to say, my sister's.

BEFORE DEPARTURE

A night I spend packing
and repacking
        until the dog falls asleep on her tail.

Daylight behind the purple curtains
        tickles my eyes. The rooster crows
in response to the dawn call to prayer.

        Mother returns
from the flea market. Brings tulips
        and sets them on a ceramic bowl of water.

Kiss her on the cheeks.
        Half-boiled eggs over rice for breakfast,
a yellow pond in the snow.

        Take me away
long enough and I will forget all this.

        Before the red suitcase drifts
from the front door to the driveway,
        one last look at the dusty framed photos:

Hindu temples on the slopes
        of a sleeping mountain; two men practicing
t'ai chi on the hills—

knees half-bent,
toes inward,
       hands as calm as the breeze;

me, a two-year old,
       hair still long, sitting on a boulder,
nibbling an unpeeled orange.

CITY OF FOUND

It's been ten years since my father sold his passport
for a basket of tithe offerings. This was before

                        there were borders and immigration
            officers, before there were islands in the streets.

I sometimes dream I hear my father crying before I sleep,
I tell the neighbors he is lost,

            but will soon come home
                        from the high tide.

It's sad to say, "I'll see you again."
I don't know if I ever will.

                        I only know
            I get to see more strangers at an airport

than a village well
gets to see in its lifetime.

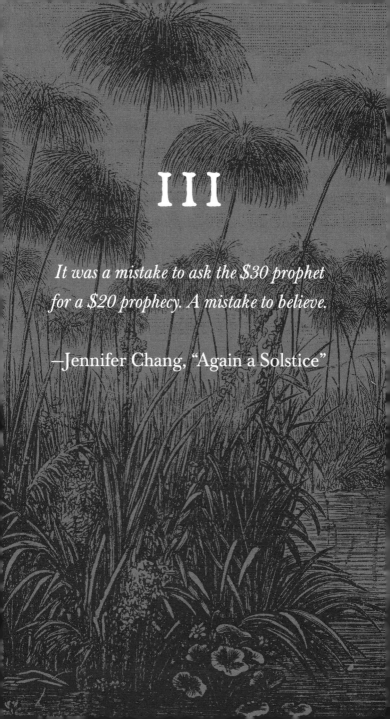

III

*It was a mistake to ask the $30 prophet
for a $20 prophecy. A mistake to believe.*

—Jennifer Chang, "Again a Solstice"

EDGE OF HEAVEN

when we were
children, we clung to
the law

we weren't meant
to touch
our bodies

there's an invisible
Maker that allows
no room for

questioning

nothing but
obedience
we begged

to stay
together
thus, our mistake

God, no longer
desires
as in heaven

the meaning of

quiet
love was lost to
the abyss because

to exist
we needed to worship
a vicious law

the
father said, yes
our greatest sin

our bodies

THE SPARROW DANCE

In the beginning   God
      started a bonfire   in the snow
        and called it lust

              We never know   what to expect
                from something that won't last

We dance   barefooted
    around the hungry flames
             sparrow and goddess

               In the cold
     the other beasts shiver in fear and jealousy:

    the red owl snickers
              retreats to its nests
the raccoon runs away to a damp cavity in a dead tree

Sometimes I put out a burning wildflower
    by swallowing it

          Here is a goddess
      that burns   Her touch stops the winter
             every night

      so her footsteps can stay
      forever

I chase her until she turns into

                          >

                        a dandelion that vanishes
            in the dark

                              and we cause
                                a wildfire

        The unfamiliar ground embraces   this lost body
              When can I call out your name
                    without having to worship you?

    All I can see now is   snow

                                      snow

                              snow

ONE ROOM

Monday

You spill your roasted chrysanthemum tea on the bed. Now the pillows smell like a field of sunflowers—I can almost hear the flight of hummingbirds in this room.

Tuesday

Biscuit crumbs all over the blankets. I try to trace your name, but I run out of crumbs. Let me go get some more.

Wednesday

Love exists here and there, like echoes. The room longs for us, all eight limbs. The room remembers our little laughers, guards them deep within four walls.

Thursday

In this room, we dance with broken shackles, the chains tapping the floors with each step. Our body sway to the rhythm of the ocean inside us.

Friday

In this room, no one can take us. We remain safe here. No voices telling us what we have is wrong, a carnal thirst. Let the sun have the protesters with their megaphones and red signs. Think of them as crows; hate is their meat, our bodies, the cadavers.

Saturday

Don't worry, we don't have to listen to anyone. Just, try to rest, for now. Later, I will part your hair, unveil sleeping your black eyes, and kiss your forehead as you dream.

Sunday

I don't know where we'll be tomorrow. But we have this room for now. As I hold you to sleep, I whisper, "This is heaven."

PROVENIENCE

I have no time to write a love poem. My plane is boarding.
They've already called my name once. I hope you understand.

I'm leaving for the last time. Yes. I know,
I say that every year. But I have to keep saying it.

This mantra reminds me that someday I will
Return home for the first time in a long time, not as a guest.

But I guess, I have always been a visitor—
either in this country or the next.

My skin tone has never been in the right shade,
nor my eyes and my tongue the right shape.

I wish I could call your country as my own.
Maybe then, I would write a love poem.

But we both know I have to leave soon.
The skies are calling my name again.

ARRIVAL IN CHARLOTTESVILLE

The freezing dawn seeps
through the bedroom window,
dispels jetlag and mirtazapine.
Bags still unpacked, don't
remember falling asleep.
The hard carpeted floor
pulses its echoes
on my back.

In my dream I was still
with you, as though there
was no reason it should be
otherwise. This unfurnished room,
its white walls—my new cage.
A friend texts me:

Is your family okay? I google
my country. An earthquake,
6.2 magnitude, a different
island than mine. This is a ritual
by now. Every year a plane crashes,
the earth consumes, a volcano
coughs, a tsunami cleanses.
I'm where I was five years ago:

in another country that will never
be mine, reading the news
about home from an empty room.
The flood recedes, the last tree in the fire
falls, we repair our roads, bury our dead.
Other than you, no longer in my life, what has changed?

THE SILENT LONGING

I boil water, make tea,
but I forget to drink.

I dice my apples
into chunks,

put them in a lunchbox,
still, I forget they exist.

I let the shower run,
their white noises

sound like indiscernible
laughter. I make and unmake

my bed, just to give
myself something to do.

I cook rice, then leave them
untouched for days.

I have leftovers in the fridge,
pizza, pasta, salad.

They stay there until
they've gone bad.

BROWN BODY

In this sea of whiteness

my body is drifting. Drifting,

for how many years now?

I look for a lighthouse

or a fisherman's boat

or any sign of a savior—

but even if I do, what then?

How to conduct this body

against the hungry waves

and the current that pulls

my veins, spins them

like a loose thread?

Mother, if you're listening

I'm still alive, alive but unsure

of my return, if ever. Please know,

where I go, the sea follows. There

will always be a sea.

ON GUILT

If the body is a temple   mine has catacombs

horses and coyotes   running in the dark

you can only tell them apart by the noise they make

one of them sounds like   footsteps in the rain

give it time and you can see their figures

in the tunnels   my mind is tired of games

empty promises   and burned bridges

If only I am good with words as I am with

silence

The stairs are wet   soon the skeletons

will sleep underwater   What would the Gods say

once they come   for their temple   now submerged

I cannot blame anyone   for my broken relationships

I am the temple with the wild horses

the coyotes   the skeletons

I pray for forgiveness   everyday

but there is no penance   for being alive

CONVERSATION WITH MYSELF AT 4 A.M.

The paper crane on my desk tilts her head a little.
I draw little circles with tails on my palm
and say, *These are fish.* She nibbles the circles clean.

Once, I've said something similar to my new therapist,
something along the lines of
These are my farewell letters. I want you to read them.

The crane flies, for the first time tonight. Looking for
   more fish, perhaps.
No more, I say. She flips my other palm, empties my bag,
and goes through my pockets, only to find letters.

See? I say. Outside, the moon sings a cradlesong,
gentle taps of rain on the empty street.
Would anyone believe me if I say pieces of my memories

got lost along the way home?
If I say, the immigration officer
prohibited me from bringing them here?

The crane gets sleepy and snuggles on my bed.
She looks like a tired martyr who can't wait to go home.
Sometimes, I lose more than memories:

A sold dog, an uncle, a best friend
married to a jealous husband, a brother turned bigot.
Home is a memory, I try to explain to the sleeping bird,

places and people change
but our memory remains the same.
When I can't sleep, I become a deer.

Sometimes, I wander around my backyard
until the river and moonlight get bored of their dance.
Right here, underneath the bridge,

is where I fold into a curl, into a memory.

MOTHER'S RECIPE FOR TONGSENG

Once the pot no longer boils,
                the child will stop tugging your shirt.

Once the stew retains its coldness
        you can begin telling it fables I once told you.

I see.

Remember the lion and the mouse with wings,
                the blind priest and your father?

I've told you all that was passed down to me.
        Yet, you are still hungry.

Yes.

Do you understand why I miss cooking
                for you?

My mother could not cook, so I promised my childhood
        a peacock that sings and a mother who cooks.

I see.

My mother loved her children
                    by sewing new dresses and trousers

out of thin fabric she'd found in the flea market,
         but not by cooking meals.

I see.

"I see" is such a strange term. Should be "I understand,"
         like an Aha! experience. Maybe understanding
is similar to the widening of a child's eyes.

ORIGIN OF CHILDHOOD

cross the oceans long enough   the land loses

its meaning   empty is the street where children
once climbed a pickup truck with both hands

or ran barefooted flying kites made
of newspaper and bamboo sticks   one day

a mother stopped waiting for her children
to come home   finished the rice all by herself

when does childhood end
and memories begin   for the first time

we start to see the beauty in being forgotten
the hushed remains of a prayer

DISBELIEF

Here,
a body,
that was
never
a body.
lonely,
he waited for
the permission
to feel the warmth
a touch,
thus cracked lips preyed
upon him as though

he was sinful,
Elders preached:
of faith
a burden,
months
full of
sacred flames,
the voice of God
in the cave,
shattered,
like
a cup—

for having
a heart
was
the burden
of all believers,
the verses,
they gave him
a command,
but not this,
thus the prayer.
the devil
was his body.

ERRATA

I'm done walking. My
faith tells me I am
exactly where my God
wants me to be.

NOTES

I:

The epigraph from John 4:44 comes from the 21st
Century King James Version of the Bible

II:

The epigraph from Kei Miller comes from *There Is an
Anger That Moves* (Carcanet Press Ltd, 2007).

III:

The epigraph from Jennifer Chang comes from
Some Say the Lark (Alice James Books, 2017).

ACKNOWLEDGMENTS

I'm grateful to the editors of the following journals where these poems first appeared, sometimes in earlier forms:

Bridge: The Bluffton University Literary Journal: "Dogma"

Cider Press Review: "Nightly Prayer"

The Cincinnati Review: "City of Lost" and "City of Found"

Columbia Journal: "Confession"

Crab Fat Magazine: "Father Abecedarian"

Ginosko Literary Journal: "One Room," "The Silent Longing" and "The Sparrow Dance"

Inverted Syntax: "Arrival in Charlottesville"

Juked: "A Prophet Without Words"

LandLocked Magazine: "A Conversation with Snow"

The McNeese Review: "Song of the Sparrow" and "Father, Forgive Me"

Poetry Northwest: "Heritage"

Prairie Schooner: "When I Came Home"

Relief: A Journal of Art and Faith: "Conversation with a Bleeding God in My Arms"

Sheila-Na-Gig Online: "Provenience"

Sigma Tau Delta Rectangle: "Altar"

Sixfold: "Before Departure"

Third Coast Magazine: "Meditation: A Memory (as prose)"

Wingless Dreamer: "Black Hole"

A river of gratitude to my teachers, mentors, and earliest supporters for my work at Western Michigan University: Becky Cooper, Nancy Eimers, SMarie Lafata-Clay, and Sara Lupita Olivares. Your belief in my voice continues to shape my words. I often revisit the myriad lessons each of you imparted.

I am thankful to the University of Virginia's MFA program for providing the substantial space, time, and support that allowed me to finish this collection. Words cannot express my appreciation for the life-altering opportunity I received.

To my wonderful students who inspire me with their stories, dreams, and passions, thank you for engaging in our shared learning journey.

To my community in Charlottesville, Christie Blonkvist, Aubrey Carley, Matt Dhilon, Eric Dominguez, Tafara Gava, Elizabeth Kim, Andie Waterman, Xiwen Wang, and Holly Zhou. Our conversations have been an endless wellspring of music and poetry.

A rain of thanks to everyone in Indonesia, my homeland, who holds my name dear. Let's eat soon. To my family there, I hope someday, you will pick up this book, read its pages, and find moments that bring laughter. To my sister, for keeping me sane.

My gratitude to the Codhill Press team; your trust and care have been invaluable. A special acknowledgment to Robert Krut for the honor of selecting my work and for your continued support long after.

I offer my thanks to the sacred divine that guided my journey into poetry, granting me liberation and revelation, and setting me on a path to explore and express my truth.

Finally, to Jingrun Lin—thank you. You make me a better person.